WOMEN WHO DARED

A Book of Postcards • Pomegranate Artbooks • San Francisco

On the front cover, left to right: Marie Curie,
Ruth Elder and Sarah Winnemucca.
On the back cover: Valentina Tereshkova.

Pomegranate Artbooks
Box 808022
Petaluma, CA 94975

© 1991 Pomegranate Artbooks, Inc.

ISBN 0-87654-807-9
Pomegranate Catalog No. A576

Pomegranate publishes several other postcard collections on
many different subjects. *Women Who Dared* are also featured
in Pomegranate calendars, cards and posters.
Please write to the publisher for more information.

Designed by Nick Valentine

Printed in Korea

*T*he images in this book recall with admiration and respect 32 women who made a positive difference in the world, for women and men everywhere. Included within are photos and short bios on women from history and today: artists and politicians, research scientists and daredevils, teachers and seekers. These individuals succeeded despite being frequently at odds with the conventions of their times, who broke with tradition as well as sexual and political tyrannies.

WOMEN WHO DARED

Pioneer Women shared the extreme hardships of settling the wilderness and were frequently the only civilizing white presence on the American frontier. Here a mother and child stand in a field of wheat near Newcastle, Wyoming.

POMEGRANATE • BOX 808022 • PETALUMA, CA 94975

Photograph courtesy Wyoming State Archives, Museums and Historical Department

WOMEN WHO DARED

Frida Kahlo (1907-1954), Mexican painter and international intellectual celebrity. She triumphed over physical injury and chronic pain to gain recognition as one of Latin America's finest painters with works of sometimes brutal honesty and self-evaluation.

POMEGRANATE • BOX 808022 • PETALUMA, CA 94975

WOMEN WHO DARED

Susan B. Anthony (1820-1906), American champion of
women's suffrage, active abolitionist and organizer of
temperance unions. She was the first—and so far the only—
woman honored by being depicted on U.S. currency.

POMEGRANATE • BOX 808022 • PETALUMA, CA 94975

WOMEN WHO DARED

Valentina Tereshkova (b. 1937), Russian cosmonaut. She became the first woman in space on June 16, 1963, aboard *Vostok VI*. She continues to hold the world record for the longest time spent in space by a woman — 70 hours, 50 minutes.

POMEGRANATE • BOX 808022 • PETALUMA, CA 94975

Photograph courtesy Soviet Life/Novosti

WOMEN WHO DARED

Rosa Parks (b. 1913), American civil rights activist. She sparked the successful 1955-56 Montgomery, Alabama, city bus boycott when she refused a driver's order to give her seat to a white man simply because she was black (as mandated by city ordinance).

POMEGRANATE • BOX 808022 • PETALUMA, CA 94975

Photograph courtesy Wide World

WOMEN WHO DARED

Indira Gandhi (1917-84), Indian politician. She became the
leader of the world's largest democracy in 1966 and for almost
22 years thereafter was the leading voice for India and the
third world in international affairs.

POMEGRANATE • BOX 808022 • PETALUMA, CA 94975

Photograph by Marcel Sternberger, © Ilse Sternberger

WOMEN WHO DARED

Marian Anderson (b. 1902), American contralto. She gained
international recognition before becoming the first black
member of the New York Metropolitan Opera in 1955.
Anderson was a goodwill ambassador for the United States
and a delegate to the U.N. She received the Presidential
Medal of Freedom in 1963.

POMEGRANATE • BOX 808022 • PETALUMA, CA 94975

WOMEN WHO DARED

Dian Fossey (1932-85), American primatologist. She was killed while engaged in well-publicized economic and political battles to preserve the mountain gorilla in Rwanda and has become a hero to wildlife preservationists and environmentalists the world over.

POMEGRANATE • BOX 808022 • PETALUMA, CA 94975

WOMEN WHO DARED

Helen Caldicott (b. 1938), Australian antinuclear activist and
pediatrician. She effectively stumps the world to educate the
public on the carcinogenic and mutagenic effects of radiation.

POMEGRANATE • BOX 808022 • PETALUMA, CA 94975

Photograph courtesy Wide World

WOMEN WHO DARED

Rachel Carson (1907-64), American biologist and writer. Her scientific accuracy and thoroughness made *Silent Spring* (1962) a powerful warning of the growing danger of unrestricted use of chemical pesticides and herbicides.

POMEGRANATE • BOX 808022 • PETALUMA, CA 94975

Photograph courtesy Wide World

WOMEN WHO DARED

Ruth Elder (1904-77), American pioneer aviator. Inspired by
Charles Lindbergh, she attempted but failed to fly the
Atlantic in 1927. Nevertheless she was treated as a hero and
went on to successfully promote women in aviation.

POMEGRANATE • BOX 808022 • PETALUMA, CA 94975

WOMEN WHO DARED

Sarah Winnemucca (1844-91), Native American rights
activist. She gained fame as a translator and negotiator for
the U.S. Army. She traveled extensively and lectured on
behalf of her people and later established a school for Native
American children in Nevada.

POMEGRANATE • BOX 808022 • PETALUMA, CA 94975

WOMEN WHO DARED

Charlotte Perkins Gilman (1860-1935), American philosopher and author. Arguably the most influential woman thinker of her generation, she was most noted for combining socialism and feminism to provide a coherent theory of women's oppression and for adding intellectual backing to the fight for women's rights.

POMEGRANATE • BOX 808022 • PETALUMA, CA 94975

WOMEN WHO DARED

Marie Curie (1867–1934), Polish scientist. With her husband she won the 1903 Nobel Prize in physics for the isolation of radium and polonium. In 1911 she became the first person to receive a second Nobel Prize, for further research into the properties of radium.

POMEGRANATE • BOX 808022 • PETALUMA, CA 94975

WOMEN WHO DARED

Laura Bridgeman (1829-89), American teacher at the Perkins
Institution for the Blind. She was the first blind, deaf and
mute person known to have been successfully taught.
Anne Sullivan (1866-1936), American teacher. After entering
Perkins Institution, surgery restored some of her sight and
she graduated at the head of her class. After studying
Samuel Gridley Howe's work with Laura Bridgeman, she
traveled to Alabama to become governess to a blind, deaf
and mute six-year-old — Helen Keller.
Helen Keller (1880-1968), American lecturer and writer. Her
efforts to improve treatment of the deaf and blind were
influential in removing the handicapped from asylums. She
was awarded the Presidential Medal of Freedom in 1963.

POMEGRANATE • BOX 808022 • PETALUMA, CA 94975

Photographs courtesy Brown Brothers

WOMEN WHO DARED

Julia Morgan (1872-1957), American architect. Most famous for her design of William Randolph Hearst's castle at San Simeon, California, she was the first woman ever to gain a certificate in architecture from the prestigious Ecole des Beaux-Arts in Paris.

POMEGRANATE • BOX 808022 • PETALUMA, CA 94975

WOMEN WHO DARED

Mary Wollstonecraft (1759-97), English feminist author. She
wrote what history has since acclaimed as the bible of the
women's rights movement — *A Vindication of the Rights of
Women* (1792). With its liberating view of women's place, this
pioneering work has influenced generations of feminists.

POMEGRANATE • BOX 808022 • PETALUMA, CA 94975

WOMEN WHO DARED

Eleanor Roosevelt (1884-1962), American humanitarian and
diplomat. She was an activist first lady who made the position
one of great, if unofficial, influence. As a delegate to the
fledgling United Nations in 1948, she played a central role in
drafting and securing adoption of the Universal Declaration
on Human Rights.

POMEGRANATE • BOX 808022 • PETALUMA, CA 94975

WOMEN WHO DARED

Dorothea Dix (1802-87), American social reformer. Despite
public apathy, disbelief and outright opposition, with dignity,
feverish compassion and determination, she directly
promoted the building of 32 mental institutions in the United
States at a time when insane and emotionally disturbed
people were routinely imprisoned with criminals and then
forgotten.

POMEGRANATE • BOX 808022 • PETALUMA, CA 94975

Photograph courtesy Historical Picture Service, Inc.

WOMEN WHO DARED

Martha Gellhorn (b. 1908), American journalist and writer.
Her journalism was constantly applauded as she covered the
human aspects of war in Spain, Finland, China, Java, Israel
and Vietnam. Her best fiction serves as a mirror, a
compelling reflection of humanity and a penetrating glance
at ourselves.

POMEGRANATE • BOX 808022 • PETALUMA, CA 94975

WOMEN WHO DARED

Elizabeth Gurley Flynn (1890-1964), American labor organizer. She lived most of her life on the lines, from strikes and free speech demonstrations to antiwar, prolabor political activities. She wrote, lectured and organized on women's issues, demanding both equal pay and protective legislation.

POMEGRANATE • BOX 808022 • PETALUMA, CA 94975

Photograph courtesy Brown Brothers

WOMEN WHO DARED

Mother Jones (1830-1930), Irish-American labor agitator. She
helped found the Social Democratic Party in 1898 and was
present at the founding of the International Workers of the
World in 1905. A little old woman in a black bonnet, in her
later years she was a compelling speaker and a fierce
adversary of capitalists and industrialists everywhere.

POMEGRANATE • BOX 808022 • PETALUMA, CA 94975

WOMEN WHO DARED

Harriet Tubman (1820?-1913), American abolitionist. With extraordinary courage, ingenuity, persistence and iron discipline (she carried a loaded revolver to encourage the timid), Tubman became the underground railroad's most famous "conductor" and was known as the "Moses of her people." Rewards for her capture offered by slave owners eventually topped $40,000. (In the photo Tubman is at left with a group of former slaves)

POMEGRANATE • BOX 808022 • PETALUMA, CA 94975

WOMEN WHO DARED

Abigail Adams (1744-1818), American. A lively and intelligent woman, she was one of the most distinguished and influential of the first ladies. Wife of President John Adams and mother of President John Quincy Adams, her detailed letters are a vivid source of social history.

POMEGRANATE • BOX 808022 • PETALUMA, CA 94975

Illustration courtesy Culver Pictures, Inc.

WOMEN WHO DARED

Ida Tarbell (1857-1944), American editor and writer. She was
a leading muckraking journalist and champion of honest
government and trust-busting. Her *History of the Standard Oil
Company* (1904) exposed the ruthless practices of big
business and the wasteful exploitation of natural resources.

POMEGRANATE • BOX 808022 • PETALUMA, CA 94975

WOMEN WHO DARED

Zora Neale Hurston (1901-60), American novelist. She was an important figure in the Harlem Renaissance of the 1920s and 1930s. Her fascination with folklore, magic and dialect are reflected in her study *Mules and Men* (1935) and her novels *Moses, Man of the Mountain* (1938) and *Seraph on the Suwanee* (1948).

POMEGRANATE • BOX 808022 • PETALUMA, CA 94975

WOMEN WHO DARED

Frontier Schoolmistresses. Blanche LaMont posed handsomely with her school and students at Hecla, Montana, 1893. Often little older than their pupils, these young teachers were frequently the only repositories of the best of western culture and civilization to be found in the wilderness.

POMEGRANATE • BOX 808022 • PETALUMA, CA 94975

WOMEN WHO DARED

Dorothy Thompson (1894-1961), American journalist.
Thompson started as a foreign correspondent and became
best known for her aggressive antifascist reporting and
commentary in the 1930s. Her books include *The New
Russian* (1928) and *Listen, Hans* (1942).

POMEGRANATE • BOX 808022 • PETALUMA, CA 94975

WOMEN WHO DARED

Isadora Duncan (1878-1927), American dancer. She rejected
the constraints of formal ballet, insisting on her own lyrical
free-form style. Her dances, based on Greek theme and
costume, shocked American audiences but were warmly
received in Europe. In 1921 she opened a dance school in the
Soviet Union.

POMEGRANATE • BOX 808022 • PETALUMA, CA 94975

Photograph courtesy Wide World

WOMEN WHO DARED

Dorothea Lange (1895-1965), American photographer.
Disabled by polio as a child, she had a lifelong sympathy with
the disadvantaged. Her photo "Migrant Woman" (1936) is one
of the most widely recognized images of the Great
Depression. Her work profoundly influenced American
photojournalism with its simplicity and directness.

POMEGRANATE • BOX 808022 • PETALUMA, CA 94975